Funny you should sing th...
THE SONGS OF
JEREMY NICHOLAS

For Jill, with love

Novello
London and Sevenoaks

Cat. No. 10 0338

Contents

Cover illustration by Clive Francis

© Copyright 1993 Novello & Company Limited

Head office: 3 Primrose Mews, 1A Sharpleshall St.,
London NW1 8YL   Tel 071 483 2161   Fax 071 586 6841

Sales: 7 Vestry Road, Sevenoaks, Kent, TN14 5EL
Tel 0732 464999   Fax 0732 459779

Funny you should sing that . . .

I was lucky. I was brought up on Gilbert and Sullivan, one of music's great song-writing partnerships. The rhythms of the words, the catchy tunes, the perfectly-placed punchlines, the ingenious rhyming schemes - all appealed to something in me very early on. Parodies (the more subversive the better) I found hugely entertaining and I quickly progressed from 'Oh dear what can the matter be, / Three old ladies were locked in the lavatory' and 'While shepherds watched the box at night / All tuned to BBC, / The angel of the Lord came down and changed to ITV' to the more risqué 'They're changing sex at Buckingham Palace: / Christopher Robin turned into Alice' and 'Puff the magic dragon lived on a shelf. / He didn't have no playmates, so / Puff played with himself'. At school I began writing my own (mainly scatological) alternative lyrics:

> We've got toilets, we've got drains,
> We're connected to the mains,
> We've got white enamel pedestals
> We flush by pulling chains
> And we sometimes get a broken hook
> To hang up all our caper.
> What don't we get? We don't get paper!

Caper/paper is a weak rhyming solution and also adds a syllable to the original tune. It gets a laugh in performance but I wouldn't allow myself to write such a cheat of a line now.

From a single 78 rpm record by the 'Blue Boy of Variety', Ronald Frankau, mysteriously acquired by my parents, I learnt that lyrics had not only to be ingenious, witty and structured but make grammatical sense. *They have a much better time when they're naughty* and the flip side *I'd like to have a honeymoon with her* were typical of the near-the-knuckle songs that Frankau churned out in the '30s, all beautifully crafted, a red-blooded Noel Coward without the benefit of Coward's potent tunes. (Another thing they had in common: a detestation of a sloppy rhyme - 'laugh' never rhymed with 'bath'.) Of all Coward's qualities, accuracy and truth in observation, and unexpectedness of rhyme and metre were his hallmarks, allied to the sheer virtuosity of lines such as:

> She declined to begin the Beguine
> Though they besought her to
> And in language profane and obscene
> She cursed the man who taught her to,
> She cursed Cole Porter too!
>   (*Nina* from *Sigh No More*)

Who else has been an influence? Flanders and Swann (*At the drop of a hat, At the drop of another hat, The Bestiary* - quintessentially English, a quality which, whatever else are their merits, I hope is in *my* songs); Tom Lehrer ('Take your cigarette from its holder / And burn your initials in my shoulder' from *The Masochism Tango* are two of my favourite lines from *any* song); and then there's Clement Wood. He's not a songwriter as such. He's the author / compiler of the best rhyming dictionary, the only one worth having.

Most of the songs in this album were originally commissioned for *Stop The Week*, a BBC radio programme which was broadcast on Saturday evenings from the mid-seventies until 1992. In 1975 my work as an actor brought me into contact with the songwriter Peter Skellern who had had a smash hit with a song called *You're A Lady*. I took over from him in *Loud Reports*, a mini-musical that he'd co-written. The friendship that ensued led me to play some of my songs to him. At the time, he was contributing two topical 'comic' songs per week to *Stop The Week* and was more than happy to introduce me to the programme. Eventually, the commission of two songs a week was reduced to one and the still-daunting work process then went like this: the producer, Michael Ember, would phone on Thursday afternoon with the subjects that were to be discussed by the guests on the programme. Chaired by Robert Robinson, these, typically, would run the gamut from 'how do you get rid of unwanted guests?', 'why are sandals wrong?' and 'the trouble with Volvo drivers' to 'why are we so bad at the sports we invented?', 'is it acceptable to floss in public?' and 'buttons or zips?'. With the subject for the song decided, the lyrics would be written on Thursday night, polished on Friday morning (along with the composition and scoring of the music) and recorded Friday after lunch. It's amazing what panic can inspire.

From 1977, for the next twelve years, Michael Ember asked me to write for the programme, alternating not only with Peter Skellern on four-weekly stints, but with the group Instant Sunshine and (later) Fascinating Aida. Both Peter and Michael have my undying gratitude.

There are other people I should like to thank now that some of the 'polished' versions of those songs are appearing in public. Don Lawson (drums), Allan Walley (double-bass) and Terry Walsh (guitar) played on most of the sessions. Through their expertise and generosity, I picked up many tricks of their trade and learnt how to score for these superb musicians; their patience, while I fumbled around at the keyboard, experimented, changed my mind, did the umpteenth take and then-re-wrote the entire thing, was boundless.

The pianist, Roger Vignoles was the first person to 'pick up' on my songs and, with the mezzo-soprano, Sarah Walker, record them. It was entirely due to him that this volume has appeared, for he presented two of my songs (*Place Settings* and *Usherette's Blues*) to Novello & Co who published them in a collection called *Sarah's Encores*. To have the encouragement of a musician of Vignoles' stature has been a source of inspiration.

I should like to thank Clive Francis for his uncannily accurate cover portrait and, finally, the person who commissioned it. One influence on my lyric writing I haven't mentioned. His name is Harry Graham, best remembered now as the creator of *Ruthless Rhymes*.

> Billy, in one of his nice new sashes,
> Fell in the fire and was burnt to ashes;
> Now, although the room grows chilly,
> I haven't the heart to poke poor Billy.

That is pure genius: the story, the economy, the rhyme, the punchline. Graham, writing these in the late 1890s, went on to become a lyricist and prolific writer of light verse. He it was who wrote the English lyrics for *White Horse Inn* and *The Land Of Smiles* (*You are my heart's delight* is his) as well as *The Maid Of the Mountains* and a host of other West End successes. I wrote a radio programme about him a few years ago in the process of which I met his daughter, Virginia Thesiger, who, as Virginia Graham, is no mean wit and wordsmith herself. To have her as a friend is one thing, but to have her connected in this way with FUNNY YOU SHOULD SING THAT... is a source of immense pleasure and pride for me.

Jeremy Nicholas
Barley Fen
January 1993

FUNNY YOU SHOULD SING THAT

Words and Music by
JEREMY NICHOLAS

1 Open Wide

*Spoken with the tongue pushed down between the bottom lip and front of the lower teeth.

2

4

(to Coda last time)

That and ci - ga - rettes in - cline to make your breath reek. _ O - pen wide, o - pen wide, o - pen
ea - si - er to find out what the hell I have hit. _ O - pen wide, o - pen wide, o - pen
sig - nal with your hand when you're be - gin - ning to choke. _ O - pen wide, o - pen wide, o - pen
up - right, rinse your mouth and spit them out in the sluice. _ O - pen wide, o - pen wide, o - pen

1

wide! O - pen wide!
wide! O - pen

D.S.

2

CODA

wide! O - pen, wide, o - pen wide, o - pen wide! O - pen

wide, o - pen wide, o - pen wide! _

gliss.

sfz

2 I Can't Quite Remember Your Name

6

Seductively (♩.= 54)

I know that we met at a
friend said your fa – ther was
know that you came back to

par – ty last year But I can't quite re – mem – ber your name. You like listen – ing to
weal – thy as Croes – us. Why can't I think of your name? You went to
my place that night But I can't quite re – mem – ber your name. You asked me to

Pou – lenc and Sat – ie– it's queer But I just can't re – mem – ber your name. I re-
Gir – ton and I went to – ge– Je – sus! Why can't I think of your name? I re-
get out and turn off the light– I *still* can't re – mem – ber your name. We

-mem - ber your scent and the touch of your lips, And the way you liked eat - ing as-
-mem - ber your birth - day, your Zo - di - ac sign, Your tel - e - phone num - ber- six
woke up next morn - ing and drank some cham - pagne And though it is love - ly to

-pa - ra - gus tips. I'm a - fraid that my mem' - ry's to blame, But I
eight dou - ble nine. But my mem' - ry has put me to shame, 'Cos I
see you a - gain, I sus - pect that you're think - ing the same, 'Cos you

⊕ to Coda

a little quicker

can't quite re - mem - ber your name. Was it Cl - eo or Cla - ra or
can't quite re - mem - ber your name. Is it Be - a - trix, Bren - da or

Chlo - e? Was it Ca - thy or Car - rie I kissed? Per - haps it was
Bri - dget? My ad - dress book I real - ly should bring. Oh it's whats - it, the

I Can't Quite Remember Your Name
(Girls Version)

Oh I say! There's that guy with Sebastian -
He's not seen me yet in this crush.
He's a man I adore - yes, I've met him before,
But there's one tiny problem I cannot ignore
And it's brought on a little hot flush...

I know that we met at a party last year
But I can't quite remember your name.
You like listening to Poulenc and Satie - it's queer
But I just can't remember your name.
I remember your smile and the touch of your lips,
And the way you liked eating asparagus tips.
I'm afraid that my memory's to blame,
But I can't quite remember your name.

Was it Alec or Alan or Andy?
Was it Adam or Angus I kissed?
Perhaps it was Dicky... or David or Derek,
I wish that I'd made out a list.

A friend said your father was wealthy as Croesus.
Why can't I think of your name?
I went to Girton and you went to - Jesus!
Why can't I think of your name?
I remember your birthday, your Zodiac sign,
Your telephone number - six eight double nine.
But my memory has put me to shame,
'Cos I can't quite remember your name.

Is it Berny or Barney or Barry?
My address book I really should bring.
Oh, it's whatsit, the whosits -
The friend of the doobies -
If I ask him I'll blow the whole thing.

I know that you came back to my place that night
But I can't quite remember your name.
I asked you to get out and turn off the light -
I *still* can't remember your name.
We woke up next morning and drank some champagne
And though it is lovely to see you again,
I suspect that you're thinking the same,
'Cos you can't quite remember my name...
I know where I met him,
I'd never forget him,
Now all I can do is exclaim:
(SPOKEN) 'Hallo, darling! How are you?'
Gosh, I hope I remember his name.

3 Camping Out

10

I be-came a Queen's Scout_ I sang this camp-ing song: Can you get your tent pole up in the
ask for is a ground-sheet_ To stop you get-ting pi...damp:
warms a fel-low's coc-kles Just to sing the old re-frain:

dark? When you rub two sticks to-ge-ther make them spark?

Shal-la-wal-ly-shal-la-wal-ly-oom-pah, Keep your wog-gle in your hand,

Shal-la-wal-ly-shal-la-wal-ly, Be Pre-pared, The camp-ing life is grand. Have you

*If desired, instead of singing a 3rd Chorus, play it on your Kazoo. If you haven't got a Kazoo, use loo paper and a comb. If you haven't got any loo paper... whistle.

ev - er man - aged put - ting up a tent In a howl - ing gale when all the guys were

bent? Snug - gled in our sleep - ing bags by the fire - side,

1,2 D.S. **3**

I will do the scout - ing— if you will be the guide. (You will be the guide).
(or end of Kazoo solo)

4. And

14

Dad Got All His Medals Out Today

Gently, dreamily ♩= 116

con ped.

mf

Dad got all his med-als out to-
Dad got all his med-als out to-

p

sim.

- day. I had-n't seen them, oh, for years and years. When
- day- He's go-ing to a ce-le-bra-tion 'do'. The

16

done his bit for King and Coun - try and the time he saw His clos - est
B B C and IT - MA and Nor - man - dy and Hit - ler Are the

friend wiped out be - fore his ve - ry eyes. The U - Boats and the Spit - fires and mach -
things that I'm un - like - ly to for - get'. So, to -

- ine guns, The des - erts and the crowds on V E day, But when I asked Dad how he got his

med - als Well, the strange thing is my fath - er would - n't say.

⊕CODA

- day, Dad put his med-als on a-gain On the an-ni-ver-sa-ry of V E day. He's

got the D. S. some-thing___ and a row of oth-ers too. How he

got them, though, he's ne-ver going to say.

5 Presidential Precedents

The Pre-si-dents of the Un-i-ted States de-moc-ra-cy en-shrine, But there's now been more than for-ty of them since Sev-en-teen-eigh-ty-nine. In fact, so ma-ny that no-one can re-mem-ber who they were- So here's a chron-o-lo-gi-cal list to which you can re-fer.

Tempo di Hoe Down (♩=168)

(In a strong American accent)

First was old George Wash-ing-ton, the man who ne-ver lied, John A-dams, Thom-as

Pre-si-dent in Eigh-ty-one was Ches-ter Ar-thur, then Came Gro-ver Cleve-land,

octaves ad lib.

Music arranged by J.N. from:– *John Brown's Body* by C.S. Hall (1861) ; *Marching through Georgia* by Henry Clay Work (1865) ; *Dixie* by Daniel Decatur Emmett (1860) ; *Stars and Stripes Forever* by John Philip Sousa (1897)

20

21

22

6 Valentine Card

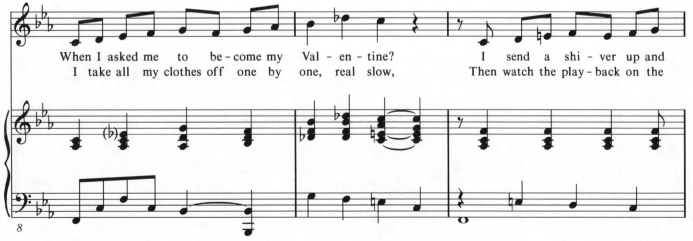

down my spine,   Can't take my eyes   off me.   De-
vid - e - o—   Can't take my eyes   off me.

- mure - ly I av - ert   My lov - ing gaze from me - it's cruel to flirt...   I
Sev' - ral in the past   Thought they'd stay the dis - tance but were all out - classed, This time it's

might get hurt.   So sim - ply, ent - re nous,   From now on I pro - mise me that
going to last.   I'm the groom and bride...   On - ly took a mo - ment for me

I'll be true, But that's not hard to do—   No long - er sligh - ted   Or un - re - qui - ted,
to de - cide and when I did— I cried.   No more temp - ta - tion,   Just pure e - la - tion

Who says that Love is blind?
Each time I catch my eye.
girl's alternative: (For I'm my own best pal)

I know my e – go
My troth's been pligh – ted.

Is my a – mi – go –
I'm so ex – ci – ted

⊕ to Coda

Oh, what a luc – ky find!

Tempo giusto

sempre legato

con Ped.

D.C.

⊕ CODA

girl's alternative: Now I'm a one guy guy.
(Now I'm a one gal gal.)

L.H.

7 Pub Crawl

1. I popped out for a drink last night down
2. Next I called in for a min-ute
3. We called in at the Lamb and Flag and
4. My friend said we should pay a vis-it

at the Bar – ley Mow, A pub – lic house with old – world at – mos-
at the Ris – ing Sun. I had a pint but did – n't like it
then the Plough and Stars And had a pint of Guin – ness at The
to the Cat and Fid – dle Where they kept a glass of ci – der in its

Erratum - Bar 32, verse 2 should read:
So we settled in the Anchor, had some lager for a change,
And played a game of darts in the saloon.

more.
tune.
Wales.
Dick,

A fel-la bought me one or two and
So I moved on to the White Horse Inn and
We went in-to the snug-ge-ry and
But we did-n't like the fruit ma-chine, the

then I bought *him* one, And then we had an-o-ther three or
then the Bull and Bush And end-ed up in-side the Fox and
half an ho-ur la-ter We had sam-pled half a doz-en of their
juke box or the beer So it was there that we de-ci-ded to be

CHORUS

four.
Hare.
ales.
sick.

1. *(Normal)* So raise your glass-es, drink a toast, God
2. *(Dishevelled and rather loud)*
3. *(Slurred with spoonerisms)*
4. *(Incomprehensible)*

Save the Queen and Cheers! Here's look-ing at you, all the best old

* alternative right hand for verse 2:

son!   Well,   bot - toms   up,   good   health,   chin - chin,   God

47

bless and down   the hatch!   No,   please,   it's   my turn!   Let   me   get   this

51

to CODA
(last time) D.S.

one.

mf

sfz

3

3

55

CODA

(SPOKEN)

"Time gentlemen, please!"

58

8 Tongue Twister

Words: Jeremy Nicholas

Music: ROSSINI
(adapted & arranged by Jeremy Nicholas)

1. If you've no-thing to do for a min-ute or two Then you might like to prac-tise your
2. In-tel-lec-tu-al smar-ties at din-ners and par-ties Will drive ev-'ry-bo-dy in-

speech. Lots of peo-ple have tried it and ma-ny con-fi-ded Sur-prise at the stan-dard they
-sane. Just by sing-ing this dit-ty they'll say, "Oh, how wit-ty-You real-ly must come round a-

32

34

-van - tage. Be - tween the ver - ses there is time for a
smi - ling and give the im - pres - sion you can do it with

sip. So ve - ry soon now you can have a quick brea - ther.
ease. And when you're fin - ished and com - plete-ly ex - haust - ed,

to CODA

What - e - ver you do, though, you must not make a slip.

D.S.

CODA

Give a shrug of the shoul - ders, take a bow and say 'Cheese! _____

sfz

pp leggiero

Published by Novello & Company Limited
Music processed by Novello using the Toppan New Scan-Note System
Printed in Great Britain